A CHILD'S BOOK OF

ART

GREAT PICTURES
FIRST WORDS

SELECTED BY
—— LUCY ——
MICKLETHWAIT

DORLING KINDERSLEY
LONDON · NEW YORK · STUTTGART

A DORLING KINDERSLEY BOOK

This book is for
Walter and Molly

Editor Elizabeth Wilkinson
Designer Mary Sandberg
Picture Researcher Milly Trowbridge
Production Samantha Larmour

First published in Great Britain in 1993
by Dorling Kindersley Limited,
9 Henrietta Street, London WC2E 8PS

8 10 9 7

Colour reproduction by CS Graphics, Singapore
Printed and bound by New Interlitho in Italy

Dorling Kindersley would like to thank the following
for their help in producing this book: Mathewson Bull,
Sheila Hanly, Richard Czapnik.

Contents

Note to Parents and Teachers

It is never too early to introduce children to art. When my children were very young, I cut pictures of paintings from magazines and pasted them on to my kitchen walls, from floor to ceiling. The most interesting I put at toddler height or within reach of the high chair. With art around the home and in the classroom, children can become familiar with it and begin to appreciate it.

Parents and teachers can have great fun learning about art with children. There is no better guide than a child, for children look at every picture with fresh eyes and honesty; they look straight into a picture to absorb what is there and they respond instinctively. To them it does not matter who a painting is by, or how important it is; the work of an Italian Master will be judged on the same terms as that of an amateur. Looking at art with children is refreshing, exciting, and often outrageously funny. As we grow older, many of us lose the ability to respond with confidence to what we see; children can help us to look again with a clear eye.

Treat these pictures as you would those in any other picture book. Look for the details, talk about the colours, discuss the clothes or the weather, or talk about how the picture makes you feel. Babies may respond to highly detailed pictures with precise lines, colours, and patterns. Young children may have fun making the noises of the animals depicted or talking about the shapes and colours in an abstract painting. Older children may appreciate the use of space in a Japanese print or the feeling of springtime in an Impressionist painting.

The history of art provides endless opportunities for discussion and for expanding a child's vocabulary and general knowledge.

In choosing the pictures for this book, I relied on instinct, on my experience with illustrated books, and on the opinions of many children who, over the years, have told me what they liked best. After much consideration, I decided that sculpture would lose too much of its magic on the printed page, so the works of art in this book are all two-dimensional.

A Child's Book of Art is a book to grow up with. On pages 62-64 there is enough information to enable the reader to find out more about the pictures and artists. As an introduction to the history of art, however, all we need are the pictures themselves. Just by looking at them, children can learn a great deal. They will spot the different paintings by the same artist, observe the differences in style and technique, and learn to put the works of art into chronological order. The precious ability to look, and see, and think for themselves must be nurtured and encouraged. With this, children can acquire a real understanding of art. Later on, they may reach out for more information in order to increase their knowledge.

Art is rich with the magic and wisdom of centuries. By opening our children's eyes to it, we can help them to understand and appreciate the world in which they live and the people with whom they share it.

The Family

The Family of Jan-Baptista Anthoine, 1664, Gonzales Coques

mother   father

children

sisters

*The Calmady Children: Emily, (1818-1906)
and Laura Anne, (1820-1894)*, c.1823, Thomas Lawrence

brothers

The Princes in the Tower (detail),
1878, John Everett Millais

brother
and sister

John Parker and his Sister Theresa, 1779, Joshua Reynolds

At Home

Bedroom at Arles, 1889, Vincent van Gogh

in the bedroom

Woman in her Bath, Sponging her Leg, 1883, Edgar Degas

in the bathroom

in the dining-room

Portrait of William Brooke, 10th Lord Cobham and his Family, 1567, attributed to the Master of the Countess of Warwick

in the kitchen

The Sleeping Kitchen Maid, 1655, Nicolaes Maes

In the Garden

A Girl with a Watering Can, 1876, Auguste Renoir

watering the plants

reading

The Garden of Paradise, c.1410, The Master of the Upper Rhine

picking fruit   playing music   fetching water

Pets

dog

Miss Jane Bowles (detail),
1775, Joshua Reynolds

rabbit

Boy and Rabbit,
exhibited 1816, Henry Raeburn

donkey

Paul on the Donkey,
1923, Pablo Picasso

kitten

A Girl with a Kitten,
1745, Jean-Baptiste Perronneau

parrot

Parrot outside his Cage, 17th century, Cornelis Biltius

Animals on the Farm

The Residence of David Twining 1787, c.1846, Edward Hicks

in the farmyard

ewe and
lamb

Cheviot Ewe and Lamb, c.1835, William Shiels

piglets

Girl with Pigs, before 1782, Thomas Gainsborough

bull and cow

Landscape with Cattle, 1895-1900, Henri Rousseau

Wild Animals

hare

The Hare, 1502, Albrecht Dürer

tortoise

Tortoise, 17th century,
from a Turkish manuscript

kangaroos
and a lizard

Kangaroos, 20th century,
detail from an Aboriginal bark painting

tiger

Tropical Storm with a Tiger, 1891, Henri Rousseau

lots of animals

The Raven Addressing the Assembled Animals, c.1590, Indian

Birds

flock
of birds

Flock of White-eyes, 1820, Satō Suiseki

cockatoo,
crane,
bullfinch,
and thrush

Indian Crane, Cockatoo, Bullfinch, and Thrush,
c.1880, Henry Stacy Marks

eagle

Eagle over Fukagawa, c.1857, Utagawa Hiroshige

geese

Two Red-breasted Geese and a Bean Goose,
c. 2550BC, detail from an Egyptian tomb painting

Fruit

a basket of fruit

Basket of Fruit, c.1596, Caravaggio

apples, pears, and grapes

Flowers and Fruit, 1865, Henri Fantin-Latour

plums, peaches, and cherries

Plums and Peaches,
17th century, Jacob van Hulsdonck

oranges and lemons

Still-life with Lemons, Oranges, and a Rose,
1633, Francisco de Zurbarán

Things to Do

reading

The Virgin (detail), c.1426-27,
Hubert and Jan van Eyck

writing

Woman Writing a Letter,
c.1655, Gerard ter Borch

drawing

The Artist's Son, Jean, Drawing, 1901, Auguste Renoir

painting

Portrait of the Artist, 1791,
Louise Elisabeth Vigée-Lebrun

Action Words

dancing

A Pair of Girls with Joined Hands Performing a Kathak Dance (detail), c.1675, Indian

The Jockey, 1899, Henri de Toulouse-Lautrec

riding

Le Plongeur, 1978, David Hockney

swimming

Footrace, c.530BC, Greek vase painting

running

swinging

The Swing, 1767, Jean-Honoré Fragonard

Counting

1

one boy

The Boy with the Fife,
1866, Edouard Manet

2

two angels

Putti from *Madonna and Child with Saints,*
c.1518, Rosso Fiorentino

3

three girls

Portrait of Three Young Girls, early 17th century, Circle of Robert Peake

4

four sisters

The Daughters of Sir Matthew Decker Bart., 1718, Jan de Meyer

5

five children

The Five Children of Charles I,
1637, Anthony van Dyck

Colours

dressed
in black

Portrait of a Girl, possibly Magdalena Luther,
c.1535, Lucas Cranach the Elder

dressed in white

Paul as Pierrot, 1925, Pablo Picasso

yellow sunflowers

Girl with Sunflowers,
1941, Diego Rivera

red room

Red Interior, Still-life on a Blue Table, 1947, Henri Matisse

More Colours

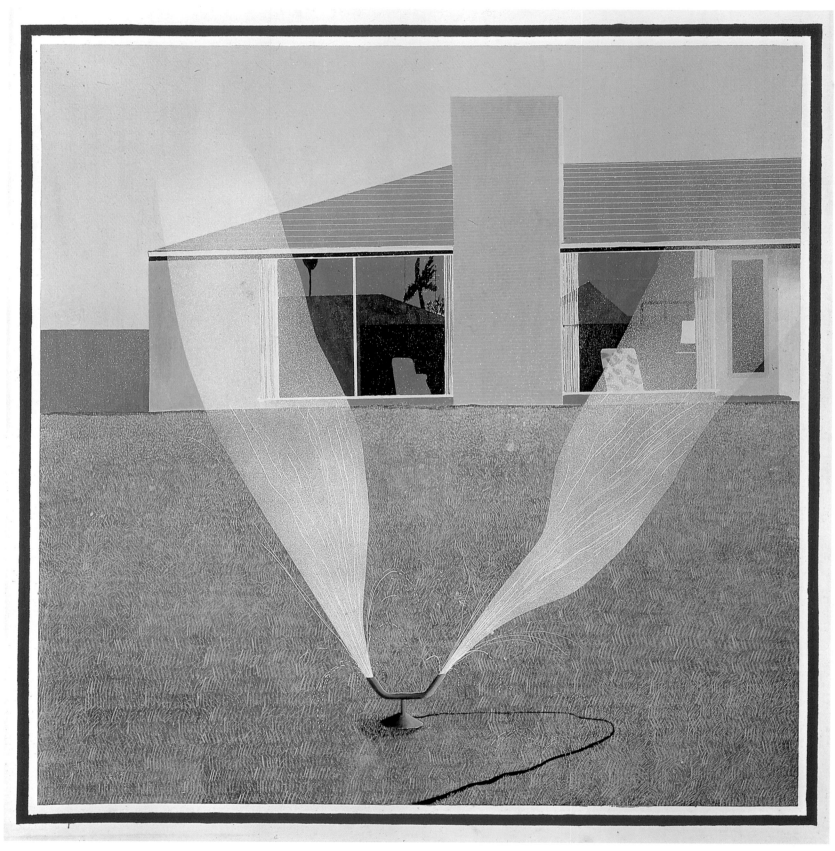

A Lawn Sprinkler, 1967, David Hockney

green grass

blue sea

Antibes, 1888, Claude Monet

lots of colours

Succession, 1935, Wassily Kandinsky

Shapes

Electric Prisms, 1914, Sonia Delaunay

circles

triangles
and squares

Composition, 1918-20, Bart van der Leck

Pompeii, 1959, Hans Hofmann

rectangles

Opposites

big and
small

Dignity and Impudence, 1839, Edwin Landseer

happy

sad

*Miniature Portraits of Two
Little Girls,* 1590, Isaac Oliver

My First Sermon, 1863, John Everett Millais

awake

My Second Sermon, 1864, John Everett Millais

asleep

young
and old

Old Man and Child,
1827, Richard Parkes Bonington

More Opposites

up
and
down
the stairs

House of Stairs 1, 1951, M. C. Escher

over and under the bridge

Evening Scene on the Occasion of the Festival of Lanterns,
c.1834, Katsushika Hokusai

The Seasons

spring

Spring, 1886, Claude Monet

summer

Wheatfield with Reaper, 1889, Vincent van Gogh

autumn

Autumn Leaves, 1856, John Everett Millais

winter

The Hunters in the Snow,
1565, Pieter Bruegel the Elder

The Weather

rainy

Sudden Shower on the Ohashi Bridge.
c.1857, Utagawa Hiroshige

Winter. 1586, Lucas van Valckenborch

snowy

A High Wind at Yeigiri, c.1830-35, Katsushika Hokusai

windy

sunny

Spring Morning, c.1875, James Tissot

By the Sea

Children Playing on the Beach, 1884, Mary Cassatt

playing in the sand

July, the Seaside, 1943, L. S. Lowry

a crowded beach

A Holiday, 1915, Edward Potthast

paddling in the sea

Faces

sideways face

The Dead King Amenophis I,
c.1050BC, detail from an
Egyptian coffin painting

mixed-up face

The Sailor, 1938, Pablo Picasso

flat face

The Brown Bear, 19th century,
detail from a ceremonial robe of
the Tlingit nation, North American

magical faces

Magical Calendar (detail), c.1300–1500, Aztec book painting

fierce face

*The Kabuki Actor Nakamura
Utaemon III in the Role of a Samurai,*
1825, Shunkōsai Hokushū

The Five Senses

hearing

The Listening Girl,
1780s, Jean-Baptiste Greuze

seeing

Mother and Child, c.1905, Mary Cassatt

smelling

Smell, 1637, Jan Molenaer

The Glass of Wine, c.1660, Jan Vermeer

tasting

touching

The Creation of Adam (detail), 1511, Michelangelo

Six Ways to Travel

The Diplomats, 1939, Peter Purves Smith

by car and

aeroplane

by elephant

A Mahout Riding an Elephant (detail),
17th century, Indian

Father Juniet's Cart, 1908, Henri Rousseau

by horse and cart

Homage to Louis David, 1948-49, Fernand Léger

by bicycle

Boston and North Chungahochie Express, after 1919, American

by train

Let's Go by Boat

fishing boats

Mount Fuji Seen Through a Fishing Net on a Clear Day,
c.1843, Utagawa Kuniyoshi

passenger boat

The Month of May, c.1540, Simon Benninck

The Owl and the Pussycat, 1981-83, Peter Blake

sailing boat

Scene on Lake Tana, showing people going to a festival at an island church, 20th century, Ethiopian

canoes

A Time to Work

October, Planting Seeds, c.1415, The Limbourg Brothers

farming

The Birth of Christ,
c.1404, Konrad von Soest

cooking

Masons Building the Wall Around the Town (detail),
15th century, from a French manuscript

building

The Country School, 1871, Winslow Homer

teaching and learning

A Time to Play

cards

The Cheat with the Ace of Diamonds, probably late 1620s, Georges de la Tour

Baby at Play, 1876, Thomas Eakins

toys

sports

The Badminton Game, 1972-73, David Inshaw

music

A Putto Musician, c.1520, Rosso Fiorentino

A Time to Eat

breakfast

Madonna Feeding the Child, c.1510-15, Gerard David

lunch

One of the Family, 1880, F. G. Cotman

dinner

The King of Portugal and John of Gaunt,
15th century, from a French manuscript

A Time to Sleep

on a wall

Man Lying on a Wall, 1957, L. S. Lowry

on a chair

Flaming June, exhibited 1895, Frederic Leighton

on a cushion

Cupid Asleep (detail),
probably 1620s, Guido Reni

on the grass

Cat Sleeping under Peonies (detail),
c.1800, Japanese hanging scroll

A Time for Peace

Peaceable Kingdom, c.1834, Edward Hicks

The wolf also shall dwell with the lamb, and the leopard shall lie down with the kid; and the calf and the young lion and the fatling together; and a little child shall lead them.

Isaiah 11:6

Picture List

The Family

6: *The Family of Jan-Baptista Anthoine,* 1664
Gonzales Coques, 1614 or 1618-1684, Flemish
oil on copper
56.5 x 73.5cm
Royal Collection, St. James's Palace, London

7: *The Princes in the Tower* (detail), 1878
John Everett Millais, 1829-1896, British
oil on canvas
147.3 x 91.4cm
Royal Holloway and Bedford
New College, Surrey

7: *The Calmady Children: Emily, (1818-1906)
and Laura Anne, (1820-1894),* c.1823
Thomas Lawrence, 1769-1830, British
oil on canvas
78.4 x 76.5cm
Metropolitan Museum of Art, New York
Bequest of Collis P. Huntington, 1925

7: *John Parker and his Sister Theresa,* 1779
Joshua Reynolds, 1723-1792, British
oil on canvas
142 x 111cm
National Trust, Saltram, Devon

At Home

8: *Bedroom at Arles,* 1889
Vincent van Gogh, 1853-1890, Dutch
oil on canvas
56.5 x 74cm
Musée d'Orsay, Paris

8: *Woman in her Bath, Sponging her Leg,* 1883
Edgar Degas, 1834-1917, French
pastel on paper
19.7 x 41cm
Musée d'Orsay, Paris

9: *Portrait of William Brooke, 10th Lord
Cobham and his Family,* 1567
Attributed to the Master of the
Countess of Warwick, working 1560-1570
oil on wood
92.4 x 119.9cm
Longleat House, Wiltshire

9: *The Sleeping Kitchen Maid,* 1655
Nicolaes Maes, 1634-1693, Dutch
oil on oak
70 x 53.3cm
National Gallery, London

In the Garden

10: *A Girl with a Watering Can,* 1876
Auguste Renoir, 1841-1919, French
oil on canvas
100 x 73.2cm
National Gallery of Art, Washington, D.C.
Chester Dale Collection

11: *The Garden of Paradise,* c.1410
The Master of the Upper Rhine
tempera on wood
26.3 x 33.4cm
Städelsches Kunstinstitut, Frankfurt

Pets

12: *Miss Jane Bowles* (detail), 1775
Joshua Reynolds, 1723-1792, British
oil on canvas
91 x 70.9cm
Wallace Collection, London

12: *Boy and Rabbit,* exhibited 1816
Henry Raeburn, 1756-1823, British
oil on canvas
102 x 79cm
Royal Academy of Arts, London

12: *Paul on the Donkey,* 1923
Pablo Picasso, 1881-1973, Spanish
oil on canvas
100.7 x 81.6cm
Collection Bernard Picasso, Paris

13: *A Girl with a Kitten,* 1745
Jean-Baptiste Perronneau, b. c.1715,
d.1783, French
pastel on paper
59.1 x 49.8cm
National Gallery, London

13: *Parrot outside his Cage*
Cornelis Biltius, working 1654-1673, Dutch
oil on canvas
60.5 x 84.5cm
Private Collection

Animals on the Farm

14: *The Residence of David Twining 1787,*
c.1846
Edward Hicks, 1780-1849, American
oil on canvas
67.3 x 80cm
Abby Aldrich Rockefeller Folk Art Center,
Williamsburg, Virginia

14: *Cheviot Ewe and Lamb,* c.1835
William Shiels, 1785-1857, British
oil on canvas
101 x 138cm
National Museum of Antiquities of Scotland,
Edinburgh

15: *Girl with Pigs,* before 1782
Thomas Gainsborough, 1727-1788, British
oil on canvas
129.5 x 152.4cm
Castle Howard Collection, Yorkshire

15: *Landscape with Cattle,* 1895-1900
Henri Rousseau, 1844-1910, French
oil on canvas
50.6 x 65cm
Philadelphia Museum of Art
Louise and Walter Arensberg Collection

Wild Animals

16: *The Hare,* 1502
Albrecht Dürer, 1471-1528, German
watercolour on paper
25.1 x 22.6cm
Albertina, Vienna

16: *Tortoise,* 17th century
Illustration from a Turkish manuscript,
translated from an earlier Arabic text
watercolour on paper
33.5 x 20.4cm (page), 5.4 x 11.2cm
(tortoise)
Jewish National and University Library,
Jerusalem

16: *Kangaroos,* 20th century
Detail from an Aboriginal bark
painting, Australian
natural pigments on bark
Private Collection

16: *Tropical Storm with a Tiger,* 1891
Henri Rousseau, 1844-1910, French
oil on canvas
130 x 162cm
National Gallery, London

17: *The Raven Addressing the Assembled
Animals,* c.1590
Illustration to a Persian Fable, Indian,
Mughal School
gouache on paper
27 x 19.4cm
British Museum, London

Birds

18: *Flock of White-eyes,* from the picture
album *Suiseki Gafu Nihen,* 1820
Satō Suiseki, working c.1806-1840, Japanese
colour-printed from woodblocks
25.8 x 17.7cm (each page) 24.5 x 14.3cm
(each image shown)
British Museum, London

18: *Indian Crane, Cockatoo, Bullfinch, and
Thrush,* c.1880
Henry Stacy Marks, 1829-1898, British
oil on canvas
122 x 81cm
Private Collection

19: *Eagle over Fukagawa,* from the series
One Hundred Views of Edo, c.1857
Utagawa Hiroshige, 1797-1858, Japanese
colour print from woodblocks
35.8 x 23.5cm
British Museum, London

19: *Two Red-breasted Geese and a Bean Goose,*
c.2550BC
Detail from a frieze from the tomb chapel of
Itet at Meidum, 4th Dynasty, Egyptian
paint on plaster
height approx. 24.4cm (detail shown)
Egyptian Museum, Cairo

Fruit

20: *Basket of Fruit,* c.1596
Caravaggio (real name, Michelangelo Merisi),
1573-1610, Italian
oil on canvas
46 x 64.5cm
Pinacoteca Ambrosiana, Milan

20: *Flowers and Fruit,* 1865
Henri Fantin-Latour, 1836-1904,
French
oil on canvas
64 x 57cm
Musée d'Orsay, Paris

21: *Plums and Peaches*
Jacob van Hulsdonck, 1582-1647, Flemish
oil on copper
28.8 x 35cm
Private Collection

21: *Still-life with Lemons, Oranges, and a Rose,*
1633
Francisco de Zurbarán, 1598-1664, Spanish
oil on canvas
61.6 x 109.2cm
Norton Simon Museum, Pasadena, California

Things to Do

22: *The Virgin* (detail), c.1426-27, from
The Ghent Polyptych
Hubert van Eyck, d.c.1426, and Jan van Eyck,
working 1422, d.1441, Netherlandish
oil on wood
168.7 x 74.9cm
Cathedral of St. Bavo, Ghent

23: *Woman Writing a Letter,* c.1655
Gerard ter Borch, 1617-1681, Dutch
oil on wood
39 x 29.5cm
Mauritshuis, The Hague

23: *The Artist's Son, Jean, Drawing,* 1901
Auguste Renoir, 1841-1919, French
oil on canvas
45.1 x 54.5cm
Virginia Museum of Fine Arts, Richmond
Collection of Mr. and Mrs. Paul Mellon

23: *Portrait of the Artist,* 1791
Louise Elisabeth Vigée-Lebrun,
1755-1842, French
oil on canvas
99 x 80.6cm
National Trust, Ickworth, Suffolk

Action Words

24: *A Pair of Girls with Joined Hands
Performing a Kathak Dance* (detail), c.1675
Indian, Mughal School
gouache on paper
22.4 x 14.1cm
Victoria and Albert Museum, London

24: *The Jockey,* 1899
Henri de Toulouse-Lautrec, 1864-1901, French
colour lithograph
51.5 x 36.3cm
National Gallery of Victoria, Melbourne
Felton Bequest

24: *Le Plongeur,* No.18 of *Paper Pools* series,
1978
David Hockney, b.1937, British
paint and moulded paper pulp
183 x 434cm
Hockney Gallery, Saltaire, Bradford.
On loan from Bradford Art Galleries
and Museums

25: *Footrace,* c.530BC
Detail from a black-figured prize amphora,
attributed to the Euphiletos Painter, Greek
terracotta
height of amphora 62.2cm
Metropolitan Museum of Art, New York
Rogers Fund 1914

25: *The Swing,* 1767
Jean-Honoré Fragonard, 1732-1806, French
oil on canvas
83 x 66cm
Wallace Collection, London

Counting

26: *The Boy with the Fife,* 1866
Edouard Manet, 1832-1883, French
oil on canvas
164 x 97cm
Musée d'Orsay, Paris

26: *Putti,* detail from *Madonna and
Child with Saints,* c.1518
Rosso Fiorentino, 1494-1540, Italian
oil on wood
172 x 141cm
Uffizi Gallery, Florence

26: *Portrait of Three Young Girls*
Circle of Robert Peake, working 1598,
d.c.1626, British
oil on wood
85 x 117cm
Private Collection

27: *The Daughters of Sir Matthew Decker
Bart.,* 1718
Jan de Meyer, b.before 1696, d.after 1740,
Dutch
oil on canvas
77.8 x 66.1cm
Fitzwilliam Museum, Cambridge

27: *The Five Children of Charles I,* 1637
Anthony van Dyck, 1599-1641, Flemish
oil on canvas
163.2 x 198.8cm
Royal Collection, St. James's Palace, London

Colours

28: *Portrait of a Girl, possibly Magdalena Luther,* c.1535
Lucas Cranach the Elder, 1472-1553, German
oil on wood
41 x 26cm
Musée du Louvre, Paris

28: *Paul as Pierrot,* 1925
Pablo Picasso, 1881-1973, Spanish
oil on canvas
130 x 97cm
Musée Picasso, Paris

28: *Girl with Sunflowers,* 1941
Diego Rivera, 1886-1957, Mexican
oil on canvas
92.5 x 74.5cm
Private Collection

29: *Red Interior, Still-life on a Blue Table,* 1947
Henri Matisse, 1869-1954, French
oil on canvas
116 x 89cm
Kunstsammlung Nordrhein-Westfalen, Düsseldorf

More Colours

30: *A Lawn Sprinkler,* 1967
David Hockney, b.1937, British
acrylic on canvas
122 x 122cm
Private Collection

31: *Antibes,* 1888
Claude Monet, 1840-1926, French
oil on canvas
65.5 x 92.4cm
Courtauld Institute Galleries, London

31: *Succession,* 1935
Wassily Kandinsky, 1866-1944, Russian
oil on canvas
78.7 x 99cm
Phillips Collection, Washington, D.C.

Shapes

32: *Electric Prisms,* 1914
Sonia Delaunay, 1885-1979, b.Russia, lived in France from 1905
oil on canvas
250 x 250cm
Musée National d'Art Moderne, Paris

32: *Composition,* 1918-20
Bart van der Leck, 1876-1958, Dutch
oil on canvas
101 x 100cm
Stedelijk Museum, Amsterdam

33: *Pompeii,* 1959
Hans Hofmann, 1880-1966, b.Germany, American citizen from 1941
oil on canvas
214.6 x 147.6cm
Tate Gallery, London

Opposites

34: *Dignity and Impudence,* 1839
Edwin Landseer, 1803-1873, British
oil on canvas
88.9 x 69.2cm
Tate Gallery, London

34: *Miniature Portraits of Two Little Girls,* 1590
Isaac Oliver, d.1617, b.France, lived in England
bodycolour on vellum mounted on card
5.1 x 3.2 cm
Victoria and Albert Museum, London

35: *My First Sermon,* 1863
John Everett Millais, 1829-1896, British
oil on canvas
92 x 76.9cm
Guildhall Art Gallery, Corporation of London

35: *My Second Sermon,* 1864
John Everett Millais, 1829-1896, British
oil on canvas
97.1 x 71.8cm
Guildhall Art Gallery, Corporation of London

35: *Old Man and Child,* 1827
Richard Parkes Bonington, 1802-1828, British
watercolour on paper
19.1 x 13.9cm
Wallace Collection, London

More Opposites

36: *House of Stairs 1,* 1951
M. C. Escher, 1898-1972, Dutch
lithograph
47 x 24cm
Gemeentemuseum, The Hague

37: *Evening Scene on the Occasion of the Festival of Lanterns,* from the series *Splendid Views of Famous Bridges of the Provinces,* c.1834
Katsushika Hokusai, 1760-1849, Japanese
colour print from woodblocks
25.7 x 38cm
Victoria and Albert Museum, London

The Seasons

38: *Spring,* 1886
Claude Monet, 1840-1926, French
oil on canvas
64.8 x 80.6cm
Fitzwilliam Museum, Cambridge

38: *Wheatfield with Reaper,* 1889
Vincent van Gogh, 1853-1890, Dutch
oil on canvas
74 x 92cm
Van Gogh Museum, Amsterdam

39: *Autumn Leaves,* 1856
John Everett Millais, 1829-1896, British
oil on canvas
104.5 x 74cm
City Art Gallery, Manchester

39: *The Hunters in the Snow,* 1565
Pieter Bruegel the Elder, b.c.1525/30, d.1569, Netherlandish
oil on wood
117 x 162cm
Kunsthistorisches Museum, Vienna

The Weather

40: *Sudden Shower on the Ohashi Bridge,* from the series *One Hundred Views of Edo,* c.1857
Utagawa Hiroshige, 1797-1858, Japanese
colour print from woodblocks
33.8 x 22cm
Whitworth Art Gallery, Manchester

40: *Winter,* 1586
Lucas van Valckenborch, c.1530-1597, Netherlandish
oil on canvas
116.8 x 198.1cm
Kunsthistorisches Museum, Vienna

41: *A High Wind at Yeigiri,* from the series *Thirty-six Views of Mount Fuji,* c.1830-35
Katsushika Hokusai, 1760-1849, Japanese
colour print from woodblocks
25.9 x 38.2cm
British Museum, London

41: *Spring Morning,* c.1875
James Tissot, 1836-1902, French
oil on canvas
62 x 40.5cm
Private Collection

By the Sea

42: *Children Playing on the Beach,* 1884
Mary Cassatt, 1844-1926, American
oil on canvas
97.4 x 74.2cm
National Gallery of Art, Washington, D.C.
Ailsa Mellon Bruce Collection

43: *July, the Seaside,* 1943
L. S. Lowry, 1887-1976, British
oil on canvas
66.7 x 92.7cm
Arts Council Collection, London

43: *A Holiday,* 1915
Edward Potthast, 1857-1927, American
oil on canvas
77.5 x 102.9cm
Art Institute of Chicago
Friends of American Art Collection

Faces

44: *The Dead King Amenophis I,* patron of the Theban workmen, c.1050 BC
Detail from the floor of the coffin of the Theban official Ahmose, 21st Dynasty, Egyptian
paint on wood
approx. 40 x 30cm (detail shown)
British Museum, London

44: *The Sailor,* 1938
Pablo Picasso, 1881-1973, Spanish
oil on canvas
60 x 50cm
National Gallery, London
Berggruen Collection

44: *The Brown Bear,* 19th century
Detail from a ceremonial robe of the Tlingit nation, North American
cloth woven from mountain goat wool
approx. 12.8 x 15.2cm (detail shown)
Portland Art Museum, Oregon

45: Detail from the *Magical Calendar* of *Codex Cospi,* one of the sacred painted books of Ancient Mexico, c.1300-1500
Aztec
natural pigments on deer-skin
approx. 18 x 18cm (section), 364cm (total length)
Biblioteca Universitaria, Bologna

45: *The Kabuki Actor Nakamura Utaemon III in the Role of a Samurai,* from the series *Famous Roles of Utaemon,* 1825
Shunkōsai Hokushū, working 1808-1832, Japanese
colour print from woodblocks
25.2 x 36.8cm
Victoria and Albert Museum, London

The Five Senses

46: *Mother and Child,* c.1905
Mary Cassatt, 1844-1926, American
oil on canvas
92.1 x 73.7cm
National Gallery of Art, Washington, D.C.
Chester Dale Collection

46: *The Listening Girl,* 1780s
Jean-Baptiste Greuze, 1725-1805, French
oil on mahogany
48.1 x 39.2cm
Wallace Collection, London

46: *Smell,* from the series *The Five Senses,* 1637
Jan Molenaer, b. c.1610, d.1668, Dutch
oil on mahogany
19.5 x 24.3cm
Mauritshuis, The Hague

47: *The Glass of Wine,* c.1660
Jan Vermeer, 1632-1675, Dutch
oil on canvas
66.3 x 76.5cm
Gemäldegalerie, Staatliche Museum, Berlin

47: *The Creation of Adam* (detail), 1511, from the ceiling of the Sistine Chapel
Michelangelo Buonarroti, 1475-1564, Italian
fresco
approx. 280 x 570cm
Vatican, Rome

Six Ways to Travel

48: *The Diplomats,* 1939
Peter Purves Smith, 1912-1949, Australian
oil on canvas
40.5 x 50.5cm
National Gallery of Australia, Canberra
Gift of Lady Casey, 1979

48: *A Mahout Riding an Elephant* (detail), 17th century
Indian, Mughal School
tinted drawing on paper
26.8 x 18.6cm
Victoria and Albert Museum, London

48: *Father Juniet's Cart,* 1908
Henri Rousseau, 1844-1910, French
oil on canvas
97 x 129cm
Musée de l'Orangerie, Paris

49: *Homage to Louis David,* 1948-49
Fernand Léger, 1881-1955, French
oil on canvas
154 x 185cm
Musée National d'Art Moderne, Paris

49: *Boston and North Chungahochie Express,* after 1919
American
oil or tempera on composition board
47 x 62.5cm
National Gallery of Art, Washington, D.C.
Gift of Edgar William and Bernice Chrysler Garbisch

Let's Go by Boat

50: *Mount Fuji Seen Through a Fishing Net on a Clear Day,* from the series *Thirty-six Views of Mount Fuji from Edo,* c.1843
Utagawa Kuniyoshi, 1797-1861, Japanese
colour print from woodblocks
23 x 33.8cm
Victoria and Albert Museum, London

50: *The Month of May,* a leaf from the calendar of an illuminated Book of Hours, c.1540
Simon Benninck, 1483-1561, Netherlandish
bodycolour on vellum
14 x 9.5cm
Victoria and Albert Museum, London

51: *The Owl and the Pussycat,* 1981-83
Peter Blake, b.1932, British
oil on hardboard
27.3 x 31.8cm
City of Bristol Museum and Art Gallery

51: *Scene on Lake Tana, showing people going to a festival at an island church,* 20th century
Ethiopian
gouache on cloth
75 x 110cm
Horniman Museum, London

A Time to Work

52: *October, Planting Seeds,* c. 1415, from the calendar of the illuminated Book of Hours *Les Très Riches Heures du Duc de Berry*
The Limbourg Brothers, working 1401-16, Netherlandish
paint on vellum
29 x 21cm (page) 22.7 x 13.6cm (image shown)
Musée Condé, Chantilly

53: *The Birth of Christ,* c.1404, a scene from the Wildunger Altarpiece
Konrad von Soest, b. early 1370s, German
tempera and gold on wood
73.3 x 55.5cm
St. Nikolaus Church, Nieder-Wildungen, Bad Wildungen

53: Detail from *Masons Building the Wall Around the Town*, illustration to *City of Women*, from the *Collected Works of Christine de Pisan*, 15th century
Illuminated manuscript, French
paint on vellum
35.2 x 28.1cm (page), 10.2 x 9.3cm (detail shown)
British Library, London

53: *The Country School*, 1871
Winslow Homer, 1836-1910, American
oil on canvas
54.3 x 97.5cm
Saint Louis Art Museum, Missouri

A Time to Play

54: *The Cheat with the Ace of Diamonds*, probably late 1620s
Georges de la Tour, 1593-1652, French
oil on canvas
106 x 146cm
Musée du Louvre, Paris

54: *Baby at Play*, 1876
Thomas Eakins, 1844-1916, American
oil on canvas
81.9 x 122.8cm
National Gallery of Art, Washington, D.C.
John Hay Whitney Collection

55: *The Badminton Game*, 1972-73
David Inshaw, b.1943, British
oil on canvas
152.4 x 183.5cm
Tate Gallery, London

55: *A Putto Musician*, c.1520
Rosso Fiorentino, 1494-1540, Italian
oil on wood
39 x 47cm
Uffizi Gallery, Florence

A Time to Eat

56: *Madonna Feeding the Child*, c.1510-15
Gerard David, working 1485 d.1523, Netherlandish
oil on oak
35 x 29cm
Musées Royaux des Beaux-Arts de Belgique, Brussels

56: *One of the Family*, 1880
F. G. Cotman, 1850-1920, British
oil on canvas
102.6 x 170.2cm
Walker Art Gallery, Liverpool

57: *The King of Portugal and John of Gaunt*, illustration from *Chronicles of England*, Volume 3 by Jean de Wavrin, 15th century
Illuminated manuscript, French
paint on vellum
approx. 45.7 x 33cm (page) 14 x 20.3cm (image shown)
British Library, London

A Time to Sleep

58: *Man Lying on a Wall*, 1957
L. S. Lowry, 1887-1976, British
oil on canvas
40.7 x 50.9cm
City of Salford Museums and Art Gallery

58: *Flaming June*, exhibited 1895
Frederic Leighton, 1830-1896, British
oil on canvas
120.6 x 120.6cm
Museo de Arte de Ponce, Puerto Rico

59: *Cupid Asleep* (detail), probably 1620s
Guido Reni, 1575-1642, Italian
oil on canvas
105.5 x 138.5cm
Private Collection

59: *Cat Sleeping under Peonies* (detail), c.1800
Hanging scroll, Japanese
ink and colours on silk
45.5 x 65cm
British Museum, London

A Time for Peace

60: *Peaceable Kingdom*, c.1834
Edward Hicks, 1780-1849, American
oil on canvas
76.2 x 90.2 cm
National Gallery of Art, Washington, D.C.
Gift of Edgar William and Bernice Chrysler Garbisch

Front Cover

From top left; clockwise:
Tropical Storm with a Tiger, page 16
The Dead King Amenophis I (detail), page 44
Bedroom at Arles, page 8
Tortoise, page 16
Miniature Portraits of Two Little Girls, page 34
Children Playing on the Beach (detail), page 42
The Artist's Son, Jean, Drawing (detail), page 23
Sudden Shower on the Ohashi Bridge, page 40
Miniature Portraits of Two Little Girls, page 34
Centre
Baby at Play (detail), page 54

Front Flap

Baby at Play (detail), page 54
The Raven Addressing the Assembled Animals (detail), page 17

Back Cover

From top left; clockwise
Tropical Storm with a Tiger, page 16
Cat Sleeping under Peonies (detail), page 59
Plums and Peaches, page 21
Tortoise (detail), page 16
Children Playing on the Beach, page 42
Boston and North Chungahochie Express (detail), page 49
Spring Morning, page 41
Sudden Shower on the Ohashi Bridge, page 40
Centre
Baby at Play (detail), page 54

Title Page

Baby at Play (detail), page 54
Le Plongeur, page 24

Contents

The Family of Jan-Baptista Anthoine, page 6
The Hare (detail), page 16
Plums and Peaches (detail), page 21
Putti, detail from *Madonna and Child with Saints*, page 26
Miniature Portraits of Two Little Girls, page 34
Winter, page 40
The Listening Girl, page 46
The Cheat with the Ace of Diamonds, page 54
Cat Sleeping under Peonies (detail), page 59

Note to Parents and Teachers

The Jockey, page 24
A Pair of Girls with Joined Hands Performing a Kathak Dance (detail), page 24
Indian Crane, Cockatoo, Bullfinch, and Thrush, page 18
Tortoise (detail), page 16
The Dead King Amenophis I (detail), page 44
Cupid Asleep (detail), page 59
Eagle over Fukagawa, page 19
The Virgin (detail), page 22
Boston and North Chungahochie Express, page 49

The author and publisher would like to thank the museums, galleries, and collectors listed for their kind permission to reproduce the pictures in this book.

Acknowledgements

The author and publisher would like to thank the following for their permission to reproduce copyright material:

pages 6-7
Coques: © HM the Queen
Millais: photo Bridgeman Art Library
Lawrence: © 1992 by the Metropolitan Museum of Art
Reynolds: © The National Trust 1991
pages 8-9
Van Gogh: © photo RMN
Degas: © photo RMN
att. to Master of the Countess of Warwick: reproduced by permission of the Marquess of Bath
pages 10-11
Renoir: © 1992 National Gallery of Art, Washington
Master of the Upper Rhine: photo Artothek
pages 12-13
Reynolds: Trustees of the Wallace Collection
Picasso: © DACS 1993 / Colorphoto Hans Hinz
Biltius: photo Bridgeman Art Library / Rafael Valls Gallery, London
pages 14-15
Shiels: © the Trustees of the National Museums of Scotland 1993
pages 16-17
Dürer: Graphische Sammlung Albertina, Vienna
Aboriginal bark painting: photo Werner Forman Archive
pages 18-19
H.S. Marks: photo Bridgeman Art Library
Egyptian Geese: photo Werner Forman Archive

pages 20-21
Caravaggio: photo SCALA
Fantin-Latour: © photo RMN
Van Hulsdonck: photo Christies
De Zurbarán: The Norton Simon Foundation F. 1972. 6. P.
pages 22-23
Van Eyck, Hubert and Jan: photo Giraudon / Bridgeman Art Library
Ter Borch: © Mauritshuis, The Hague, inv.Nr. 797
Vigée-Lebrun: © The National Trust 1991
pages 24-25
Hockney: © D. Hockney / photo Bridgeman Art Library
Greek amphora: © 1993 by the Metropolitan Museum of Art
Fragonard: Trustees of the Wallace Collection
pages 26-27
Manet: © photo RMN
Fiorentino: photo SCALA
Circle of Robert Peake: photo Sotheby's
Van Dyck: © HM the Queen
pages 28-29
Cranach: © photo RMN
Picasso: © DACS 1993 / © photo RMN
Rivera: reproducción autorizada por el Instituto Nacional de Bellas Artes y Literatura / photo © Christies
Matisse: © Succession H. Matisse / DACS 1993
pages 30-31
Hockney: © D. Hockney / photo Tradhart

pages 32-33
Delaunay: © ADAGP, Paris and DACS, London 1993
Van der Leck: © DACS 1993
Hofmann: © Estate of Hans Hofmann
pages 34-35
Millais (both paintings): photos Bridgeman Art Library
Bonington: Trustees of the Wallace Collection
pages 36-37
Escher: © 1951 M.C. Escher / Cordon Art-Baarn-Holland
pages 38-39
Van Gogh: Vincent van Gogh Foundation / Van Gogh Museum, Amsterdam
pages 40-41
Tissot: photo Sotheby's
pages 42-43
Cassatt: © 1992 National Gallery of Art, Washington
Lowry: reproduced by courtesy of Mrs. Carol Ann Danes
Potthast: Friends of American Art Collection, 1915.560, photograph © 1992, The Art Institute of Chicago. All Rights Reserved.
pages 44-45
Picasso: © DACS 1993
Tlingit ceremonial robe: photo Werner Forman Archive
Magical Calendar: photo Werner Forman Archive
pages 46-47
Greuze: Trustees of the Wallace Collectiion
Molenaer: Photograph © Mauritshuis, The Hague
Vermeer: Photo Jörg P. Anders © BPK, Berlin 1992
Michelangelo: Photo © Nippon Television Network Corporation Tokyo 1992

pages 48-49
Rousseau: © photo RMN
Léger: © DACS 1993
Anon. American painting: © 1992 National Gallery of Art, Washington / photo by José A. Naranjo
pages 50-51
Blake: © Peter Blake / photo Bridgeman Art Library
pages 52-53:
Limbourg Brothers: photo Giraudon / Bridgeman Art Library
Konrad von Soest: photo Bridgeman Art Library
pages 54-55
De la Tour: © photo RMN
Eakins: © 1992 National Gallery of Art, Washington
Fiorentino: photo Bridgeman Art Library
pages 56-57
Cotman: The Board of Trustees of the National Museums and Galleries on Merseyside
French MS: photo Bridgeman Art Library
pages 58-59
Leighton: photo Bridgeman Art Library / Maas Gallery, London
Reni: photo Christies
pages 60-61
Hicks: © 1992 National Gallery of Art, Washington

Every effort has been made to trace the owners of copyright material, but we take this opportunity of apologising to any owners whose rights may have been unwittingly infringed.